The Stations

By RL Lane

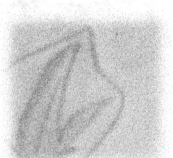

Illustrations by RL Lane

Cover Design by RL Lane

"He appeared out of nowhere. Standing there eagerly waiting for me. I told him to take a seat. Are we not yet ready to talk about the homeless? Have I not seen enough of them between NYC and Boston? He seemed happy. Most likely because he no longer needs to worry about having a home for his body. I am glad he can have the intro to this book. I called him Larry. I don't know a Larry. Oh my God...yes I do. He recently passed away..." RL Lane

I saw a purple dress with a puffy bottom like the old dresses from the 1920s, but it seemed like a modern version of those dresses. It did not go all the way to the floor. It was only knee length. It was my daughter's dress and then they said Father Jeremy or Jeremiah. We do not know a Father by that name. That dress does not seem like anything my daughter would wear unless she was dressing up for a costume party or to perform in theatre. We'll see if it and the Father cross our paths one day…

The book title is not about the Stations of the Cross, but it is Sunday today. It reminded me of dressing up in your "Sunday best" to go to church. Hardly anyone dresses up these days. Jeans and a t-shirt are acceptable attire. I miss dressing up for church. It was a sign of respect. I can still remember my Dad wearing his crisp white shirt and suit. I can still see him with the cloth shining his shoes with the black polish…

"Shoe Shine…Shoe Shine…", he used to yell. The old man at the Staten Island Ferry. He slurred the words most likely because he was tired of saying them all those years. I never did get a shoe shine. I thought it was only for guys. There is a shoe shine place in the Port Authority that I walk by every day. I am going to get my shoe shine one day soon…

The night of the purple dress they said something about Raffaele's rolls of gold. Are they still talking about the gold he buried at his son's house? I don't know why. It would be very hard for me to convince the people that live there now to dig up their yard in search of gold that I only know is there because of messages in a dream. What would that conversation look like? "Hello, I am an author. I write about things that cannot be explained. I had a dream about the Doctor and his family who previously owned your house. They said in the dream that they buried gold in the yard and it is still there." I don't think I could have that conversation. I could just send them a copy of this book. They live on Chapel Street...

The stations, like I said, are not the Stations of the Cross. They are the stations in the city. I had taken the bus from the city to Boston. It returned to the New York City Port Authority at 2:30 in the morning. I live in New Jersey. I thought the trains to New Jersey left from Grand Central Station. I walked over there only to find they had closed their doors at 2:00am. I was surprised that station is not open 24 hours. I hadn't been inside it in years and was looking forward to seeing it again. It is so easy to see the past inside those walls. A guy by Grand Central told me I needed to go to Penn Station to get the New Jersey trains. I walked back up to 7th Avenue and down to 32nd Street. There were still a lot of people out on the streets. I wondered how many of them were sober. Penn Station was open but the trains to New Jersey had stopped running until the morning. I was glad to be inside at least. I sat on my suitcase and looked around. The Boston homeless seem to be in better shape than the New York City homeless. I wonder why. There were people yelling. I come across someone yelling or fighting on the streets of New York almost every day I work there. I noticed there was no yelling in Boston in the middle of the night or the day. I wonder why…

I had to wait for the trains to start back up so I could get home. I had a home. I just couldn't get to it. It made me feel homeless for a few hours. Those few hours made me never want to be homeless. What happens when the homeless get sick? Lying in a bed sick is bad enough. Lying on hard cement or hard cold cement when you are sick is nothing I ever want to do. It seems there are more homeless men than women. Why is that? One guy was wearing a suit but it was very dirty. He would lift up his pant legs to itch his skin. Another guy had just a long coat. He would lift up his coat to scratch his itchy skin. He had no pants on, but at least he had underwear. The city doesn't let the homeless stay in the Port Authority. You have to have a ticket if you are in the waiting area. The city lets them stay in Penn Station as far as I can tell…

I kept praying that I could get back home. I used my last dollars to buy the one-way ticket home. I worried that the train would not come even though the schedule said it would start again at 7:11am. I worried that I would not get the right transfer and would be stuck someplace else. I just wanted to get back home and climb back under the covers of my bed…

This story is not about the Stations of the Cross. Those are about his last steps to a destiny he already knew. It was about the people who did not help him. He got there anyway. He made it to the end. His every step led him to that better place. He only stepped on this rock for a small number of years, yet look how much we still write and talk about him. He never published anything as far as I know. Do we even have any of his written word?

The Library of Congress says we will continue to preserve the written word in physical books like we have for hundreds of years. They say hard drives will fail and will be something else anyway. External drives blink out and are not reliable. We need our words to still remain so the people after us can learn from us. Is that why we needs our words to remain?

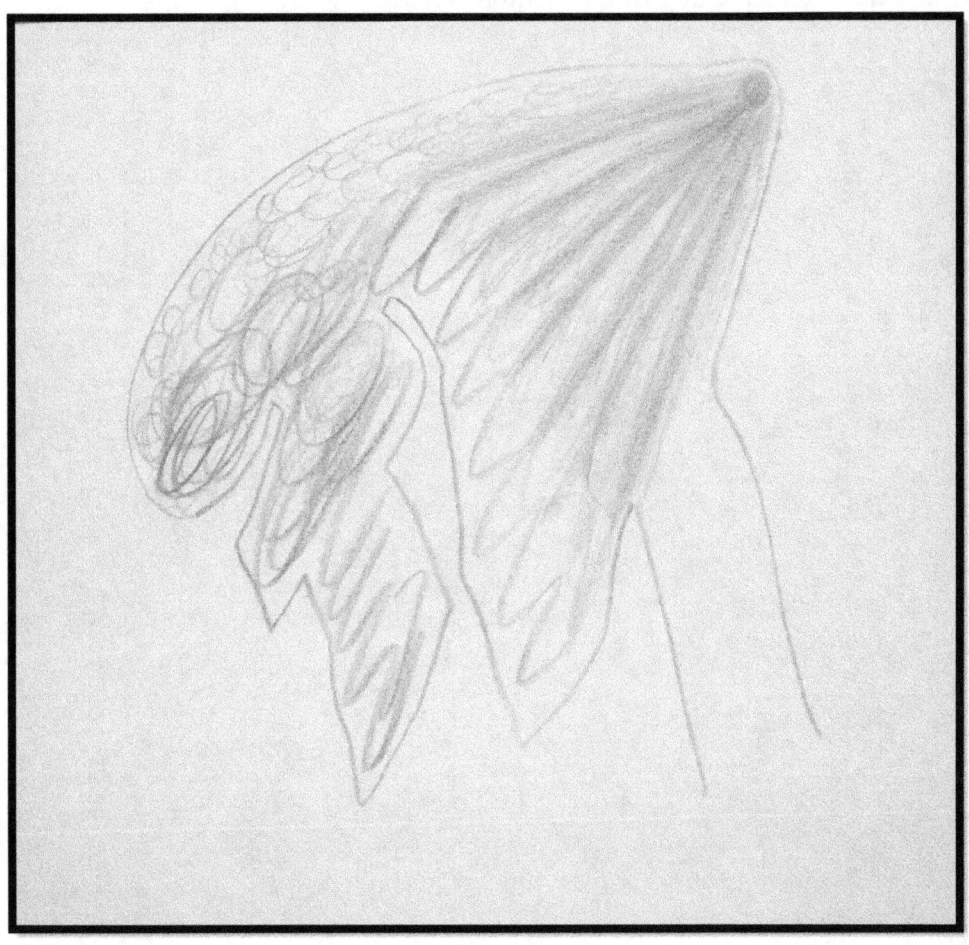

The Stations

They blamed him and cursed him

They stripped him and beat him

They made him walk with the cross

they would hang him from

They hung him up

to endure the pain

Then he died

But he went to the gates

of heaven

He prevailed

They did not

They went to the fires

He prevailed

They did not

Because

They did not

believe…

I was walking by it when I realized that is what the stations are. The baseball field "stations". Stepping on each bag as we run around the bases. I stopped to take the pictures. Front and back...

He did love the games. My Dad. Steee-rike the ump would yell as the bat swung through the empty air. Crack was the sound when the ball did connect with the wood…

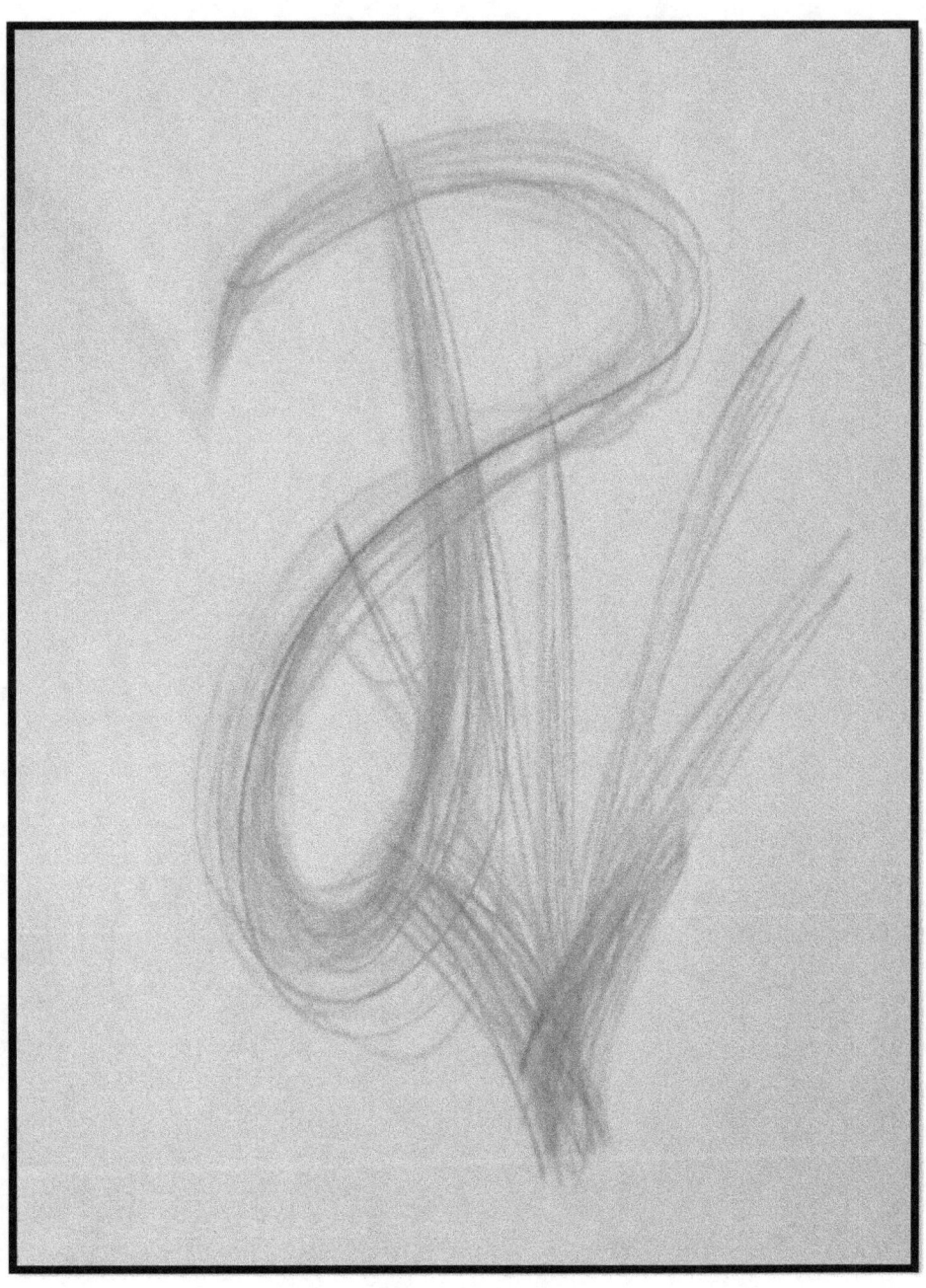

Feet pounding on the dirt as the runner tried to make it to the first station. Could they steal to the second if only they made it to the first?

My great-grandfather Anton insists he had something to do with the construction of that original Yankee Stadium back in 1922. It is something you would want known if you had been part of it. Thomas Alva developed the durable concrete that formed the stadium walls. Anton was a brick mason and he did invent a kiln. It does seem possible that he could have had a hand in the construction too…

I wonder why they invented the steal? Did nobody even back then like to play the games fairly? Steal a base when no one is looking. Steal a dollar when the purse is left open. Steal a love when the lover drops the ball...

Perhaps they should think again about the rules of the game...

Perhaps they should try to get around all the bases without having to steal…

About the Author and Illustrator

RL Lane has published the EcarreT series and a collection of short stories featuring the illustrations, along with the children's books "G" and "How to Catch a Goast". The series begins with "Chapel Street Signs"…

…unexplained connections that challenge us to beli ve. A woman, a Dad a Doctor, a cat and mouse, a horse and tale tell their stories. "Do you beli ve in spirits?" I asked my friend. "Well look", he said, "I believe there are things that cannot be explained…" Oh. Plus, hear ov a Mom's battle with her struggle to connect to the woman…her little girl.

Welcome to EcarreT…a world
Where everyone cares
Why did I have to create it in…

A fiction fantasy world?

You may already know why, but you will see regardless of what you believe as a girl's journey of love and faith on her "Touring Machine" take her on the best journey of her mundane life. A life well on its way takes a turn in a direction that could've never been seen or even dreamed…

The author can be contacted at:

RosaLeeeLane@gmail.com
www.Amazon.com/author/readrllane

Twitter.com/readrllane

Books by RL Lane

EcarreT Series:

Chapel Street Signs
secret Life OV an antE
Sri Town
Which of EcarreT

Hand of Heven

Bells to Believe

Short Stories:

Mon Treal, The Odd Cod, The Half Day, No Gift for Greed, Aunt Elm & Uncle
Poc, What Would Caitlin Wear, The Bag of Scribbles, Mr. Uraly's Italy, A not G,
Johnni and Georg, A Cup of Butter, The Walk of a THOUSAND Moods, Storm
Window, The Rugs, Cones of Ice Crème, Angel-A, The Art of Sri Town, Under
Water, The Dinner Party, The Vault, No Lines to Erase, Rock of Snow, Spilled
Sugar, A Rug and a Bag, Polka Dot Rain Boots

Children's:

G

How to Catch a Goast

Coming Soon

Bubble ov lOVe

www.ingramcontent.com/pod-product-compliance
Lightning Source LLC
Chambersburg PA
CBHW080629180526
45168CB00007B/3097